I SURVIVED

Courageous Stories of the Overcomer

Ikisha S. Cross

Ikisha S. Cross

I SURVIVED: Courageous Stories of the Overcomer

Copyright © 2021 Ikisha S. Cross

P.O. Box 882

Cleburne, Texas 76033

Published by Judiyah Publishing Co.

Edited by Darcella Perkins - RMJ Editing and Manuscripts

Cover Art Design and Illustration Concept by Kirklin Cross Jr.

All rights reserved. No portion of this book may be reproduced, scanned, stored in a retrieval system, transmitted in any form or by any means electronic, mechanical, photocopy, recording, or any other except for brief quotations in printed reviews without written permission of the publisher. Please do not participate in or encourage piracy of copyrighted materials in violation of the author's rights. Purchase only authorized editions.

Unless otherwise indicated, all scriptural quotations are taken from *the King James Version of the Holy Bible.*

ISBN: 978-1-7374135-0-9

Printed in the United States of America

Table of Contents

1. Introduction..1
2. I SURVIVED: Homosexuality............Jennifer Elaine........................3
3. I SURVIVED: Waiting ....Peggy Cross.........................11
4. I SURVIVED: Abuse.........................Dr. Veleria Coley..................19
5. I SURVIVED: Addiction..................Dr. Sariah Beatty..................27
6. I SURVIVED: Depression................Ikisha Cross.........................37

Introduction

This book is filled with the testimonies of Courageous women that have overcome insurmountable obstacles. They each share their journeys and they share their truths; Some raw and uncut. This is not a book of anecdotes or good sayings. This book is a book of traumas, habits, hurts and the road map of healing that in some cases are still taking place.

This is not an opportunity to discuss the "mess" in this book, but it is an opportunity to find the message in someone's suffering. These women have poured out their hearts and thrown caution into the wind. RESPECT THAT! They have revealed their scars so you don't have to continue to hide yours. Our prayers for this book of testimonies are for to you gain courage, motivation and divine inspiration.

I SURVIVED:
Homosexuality

As a child, I was very naïve about the world around me. From what I remember, I was a "happy-go-lucky" young lady who had a few health issues that began around age six. My parents noticed a growth on my leg, and I had a biopsy done on that tissue. I had several tumors in my right leg and in my left ankle. It was then that I was diagnosed with Campanacci's Disease and my life would take a drastic turn. After being diagnosed, I was using a walker and I needed assistance back and forth to school with my personal belongings. I had a friend at the time that I considered my "best friend" that volunteered to help me. I'm not quite sure why I considered her my "friend". I think when you are that young, you don't have a real context of what a friend is, she had never shown me anything other than being a genuinely caring person. Once again, that could have been my naivety thinking for me. Shortly after this transition to I was attacked by the very person who was claiming to be my "friend" and some of her friends at a sleepover at her house.

As I removed my body from an off-white tub, in a dark house, in a bathroom, serving as a panic room, I began to panic. My mood was frantic, I saw my friends' brother watching me bathe through a crack in the door. My life was about to change some more. I walked out, wet towel in hand. I walked into the room and my towel fell from hand. One girl grabbed me and pushed me down on the bed. Another two held me down on the bed. I'm sure they did just what she said.

I'm sure they did just what she planned; When to cover my mouth, where to place their hands. When to remove my clothes, where my body should land. I didn't understand, my confusion was as potent as the builders of the Tower of Babel They could no longer comprehend, and

I could no longer comprehend. I received the touch of man, officially reduced to second hand. I laid. I shed. I cried. I died. Or was I just stolen?

I would continue to wonder, why I was chosen.

This was my first encounter with molestation. It was a cycle that would continue through middle and high school. It's the cycle that shifted my life from bad to worse, sad to thirst, thirsting for another identity, thirsting for another me.

I began to find myself hating myself even more than the day before. I hate my body! I hate my voice! I hate that I'm a girl! I hate that I'm weak! I hate that I'm a weak girl! I wish I was a boy! "WHY do men like me?" I hate men! These and so many more thoughts plagued my mind, I couldn't understand why a grown man would mess with me? A man lurking outside my window in my gated townhouse community waiting to steal another piece of me. Why would the quarterback volunteer to help me but abuse me on the elevator? Two guys, one disabled girl, one elevator, no camera. I was defeated. Why would a teacher's assistant that I reported an incident to, tell me "The principal won't believe you anyway if you tell"? It was the church boy that I knew from the church house that would find me at school and damage my mouth. I was defeated! So many questions, so many hurts, so many incidents. Does anyone see me? Does anyone even care? What am I worth?

You would think that tears would have fallen as I cut my arms, my wrists and shaved the skin off my leg down to the white meat, so I would continue to bleed. I Rammed my head into the iron bars of my bunk bed and the walls of my room until I had a concussion. I caused my own short-term memory loss all to be "the boss" and be able to control my own pain. You would think that would have hurt me, but nothing matched what they took from me. My innocence, my joy, my identity. Thinking back now, I just wanted to be FACELESS. I felt like an unseen martyr for a cause that didn't exist.

I remember winning a drawing contest once while in school, my artwork depicted me with two faces. One half of my face on each side, separated by a crooked line. That was me showing the breakdown of how I felt on the inside. I was riddled with insecurities and filled with the desire to be a boy, a man, who would one day be with a woman. I mean life cannot be this messed up, this is a mistake. Feminine bodies are so easily broken, me I can remake. MAKE, fix it, fix she, fix and turn she to me. I'll fix it and turn she into he!

I am not sure how old I was when I began to refer to myself as George, I asked others to do the same. To my surprise, some did even people way older me.

I was 12 or 13 when *"Boys Don't Cry"* starring Hilary Swank as Brandon Teena came out. I'm sure I balled my eyes out but finally felt that I learned the language for what I was going through. A young female - to - male transgender. The tears just kept coming, that familiar heartache helped reassure me in who I thought I was, George.

Throughout that "great awakening," I began to have even more willing sexual encounters with other females. I wasn't a stranger to the female body as I had become familiar with it as I experimented with other girls in elementary and middle school. It went from just "having some fun" to "this is my desire." I know now that lust was feeding me and adding to the desires that were already inside of my head. By the time I was in 10th or 11th grade, lots of people assumed or knew I was gay. I didn't openly proclaim it but I'm sure my attire gave it away sometimes. Of course, every gay girl didn't dress like a boy but I did. I was most comfortable in baggier clothes, hiding my weakness. I graduated and was finally able to cut my hair. I was so happy. I remember being 18 or just about to turn 18 and a young lady calling me "daddy" for the first time. That fed that desire in me to be a man.

Over the years, I continued to live my life as a homosexual. People would see me and think I was a boy. I was small in stature and barely weighed 98 pounds. I was addicted to cocaine, pills, and alcohol. I started and ended my day high. It was how I was able to cope with my life. I lived "numb."

I grew up in church, but the church never really helped me heal. Rather I was abused on church property and saw the abuse of others as well by leadership so what had church done for me other than aid in facilitating my abuse? I knew God was real, but I began to blame Him and say that He made a mistake in making me a girl and I will take steps to remedy the situation.

I would bind my breasts and use a device to pee standing up. I only needed a couple more sessions to be approved to begin using the testosterone I desired to take of FOR YEARS. I was elated to have the support of my girlfriend, who I had been with for about four years, and my closest friends. I was going to fix me. I would be happier. Right?

Let's fast forward some. I began to cheat on my girlfriend after assuming she was cheating first. She found out and ended up attacking me as I came out of the restroom one night. Keeping in mind that she weighed more than twice my little 100-pound self, I didn't feel safe enough to stay in that house that night, so I left. I went to be with the new "boo." Things weren't the same and we eventually departed ways.

I began to go through a severe depression. Being high couldn't fix the way I was feeling. Plus, the new boo did not like men so I knew she wouldn't accept any parts of me having a sex change. I eventually went to Florida to visit my best friend. I got a job and a DUI on the very first weekend there. I believe the whole experience was a sobering moment for me. As I began to self-harm and bang my head into the cop car window, I recall someone in the front, maybe the cop's girlfriend asking, "What's wrong with her?" They had to call a separate cop to help bring me in. They put me on suicide watch that night. I was alone in a dark gray room naked with nothing in the room. I was balled up, cold, and out of my mind. Alcohol tends to bring out the worst. My friend's dad came and got me out of jail. No job, no identification, and no hope. I was in a very bad place.

I called a saved couple that were still my friends through all of what I was going through. They always spoke life into me. Even though they didn't agree with my choices. They always spoke to me in love and I appreciated that.

I stayed in Florida for a little while, then returned home to Tennessee. I found myself beginning to watch Christian poet sets on YouTube. One video was of a young lady who used to live a homosexual lifestyle. It was so inspiring and just what I needed. I began to look up testimony videos of those who had been freed from the lifestyle that I was embracing. The conviction came in after a while. My saved friend said "Nothing is going to change until you surrender", In so many words. I knew she was right, I decided to move in with my family.

I rededicated my life to the Lord a short while after and began to go through healing and deliverance. We were at a ministry that focused on intercession, prayer, healing and deliverance. We are byproducts of that environment and I am forever grateful.

I struggled a bit on and off with masturbation and fornication, thinking I was strong and fell headfirst right towards the beginning of walking out my deliverance.

The worst fall was about two years in, I started making bad choices. They began with hanging around one of my exes. I began to drink wine while watching a couple of those primetime shows and it went downhill from there. So far downhill, I wanted to kill myself because of some of the things that happened due to the choices that I made. That whole backslidden process lasted about 4 or five months.

I literally found myself saying "Do I want God, or would I rather have this female in my life?" The answer was God. It was a hard answer! But it was worth it. I have been sober in my identity since then.

I must remind myself to cast down vain imaginations when they try to rise. Bringing every thought into captivity as the word says. Remembering to keep my eyes on God, the One who kept me when I didn't care.

So, I'm coming out!

I have survived depression, anxiety, molestation, rape, drug addiction, gender dysphoria, homosexuality and much more. I survived so I could walk others through as well. If God can change a drug addicted transman into a minister of the Gospel of Jesus Christ, He can do anything. It's not might, nor by power, but by His spirit. And through the Blood!

We overcome by the blood of the lamb, & the word of our testimony. This is part of my testimony.

Signed,
An Overcomer

I SURVIVED:
Waiting

Mothers are the most loving human beings on the earth. They are selfless caretakers and nurturers. Mothers will go the extra mile for her children. When you think you are doing well for your family, such as; providing for them, they are in school, you are cooking and washing their clothes. You are even speaking life into them. Just good common sense talks and biblical instruction and helping them solve social problems. One problem after the other is being solved either socially or financially, or emotionally.

But the enemy still has a plan to wreak havoc on your family. the enemy can change the course of your life without you realizing it. The storms will come like a tornado or hurricane.

It will have you stretched out before God's altar. The storms will have you praying day and night. Crying unto god, wondering "How could this happen to us, to me."

Beware parents, your children will not tell you everything. They will try to hide so much from you, more than you can imagine. They will not tell you when they had in-school suspension, or got caught stealing, or fighting. They will not tell you when they had their first sexual relationship with a girl or boy. They will not tell you when they had that first puff on a blunt or a cigarette.

But today I am a surviving mother. After 45 years of marriage;

I am still finding out some of the things that happened to my children, and situations they got themselves into.

Maybe they loved me so much and didn't want my husband and I to know all the terrible details of some of their battles, or they thought he/she could handle it all by themselves.

I'm sure we all have survived the storms of life, because we have God in our lives. Are you a survivor?

Survivor means that you made it through a physical, emotional, and spiritual battle. Whether you battled well or whether the battle was more than you could take sometimes, you survived. You are alive. Surviving means adjusting to life after battle scars.

I remember the day when I was a worrier, I worried about all of my children, more about my oldest son. I was so afraid that he would get killed. We were going about our everyday life, doing what we knew to do. Trying to have a normal family, loving the children, taking them to school, disciplining and chastising them, taking them to church, praying for them and instructing them in the ways of the Lord. Then suddenly, the enemy came in like a whirlwind. I felt my life was turned upside down and out of control. My fourteen year old son started being rebellious, breaking things, and punching holes in the wall.

Where did all of this bottled-up frustration come from? What did I do? What did my husband do? Did we nurture him enough? Did we show him enough love? We were so busy working, trying to earn an income to pay bills and make life better for all of our children. Kirk and I knew it was hard times financially for us. But, we failed to consider our children's emotional health during these busy times. I assumed they understood mom and dad had to work and were busy trying to keep the household together.

Children think parents are too strict in raising them. We thought we were protecting them from the evil by teaching them to be a Christian and going to school. Yet, the peer pressure of other children was pulling them away from family and doing what they were persuaded to do.

What we didn't know was that my son had been molested as a young boy. All his frustrations were bottled up in his anger. The person told him he would kill him and his parents if he told anyone.

Then my son got older and started skipping school. All of the teachers were calling us about Kirk, Jr., our fourth child. I would cringe when the phone rang. I prayed and prayed, and sought God for answers.

One day, my son came to me very disturbed about a dream he had. He had a dream that he was out "in the streets," (doing drugs and getting involved in criminal activity), and then he returned to God and led most of his friends to the Lord. My instant reaction to that was to pray for him, which I did. I tried to dismiss my son's dream. I didn't want it to happen… but it did.

When Kirk Jr was in 8th grade, we were called to the school to discuss his behavior We had parent/teacher conferences often because of Kirk's bad behavior. We later found out that he was arrested for stealing. He would stay away from home for several days, we later realized he had been sniffing cocaine and meth, and later selling crack at night. The drugs he sniffed kept him awake, which he became addicted to.

Later we heard he was trading guns for drugs and kept guns for protection from other dealers, and people trying to steal his drugs. One thing led to another. Years later he was arrested and sent to county jail.

He was released from jail after being there for several months. He had to make up those missed school days he accrued while in jail, and attend school through an alternative education program. The teachers at Team School was saying so many good things about him. How he was so smart, and helping other students with their school work.

During that time, we found out that he was stealing his sister's jewelry and stealing our van while we were asleep. He even had guns in it! He thought he was a "gang banger" or part of a mafia or something. Crazy! It's like things were better, but then they were worst.

Throughout all of this "dark season," I felt betrayed, lost, angry, broken and confused. I also felt like an unfit mother because I couldn't seem to fix it. I knew that God wanted all of my children to be living for Him, so Kirk and I made sure that we were training up our children in the way they should go. How could this be happening to us...to me? I wanted all of my children to live a Christian lifestyle, but it seemed like there was something like a force pulling us in another direction.

I know now that being a Christian was our choice for them, not their choice to love and serve Jesus.

I started blaming myself and my husband. We argued and thought one of us should have an answer to solve this problem. Neither of us did, we both ached inside.

I realized that the devil was not playing with our family and he wanted to take my family out! Christians or not, I could just hear him laughing saying, "Where is your God now? I got your son, and I'm coming after all of them!"

I began praying more; in the middle of the night, on the way to work, fasting more, reading the Bible, praying in tongues, praying in English, praying the scriptures, and anointing Kirk, Jr. with oil when he was at home sleeping.

I began to notice more and more a change in his words and character. I saw his pupils dilated from the drugs, using street slangs, sleeping with women older than him, and wearing chains around his neck like "Mr. T." The use of cocaine and meth stimulated his sex drive. I became a prayer warrior and soldier for Christ, and I went to war for my son!

Inviting God to Work

I could no longer recite 2-minute prayers, I knew that no one else loved him like I did, except GOD. I needed some anointed, dynamite, fervent prayers for him that brought change. I was determined to get my son delivered from drugs, and fornication, and not have the other seven children follow in his direction of sin. I knew this was not a fight against flesh and blood, but against evil, principalities, powers, and rulers of darkness. I know that my husband was praying, but I felt that I needed to know God heard me.

We loved him so much, We loved all of our children. This was a season that I couldn't consider myself. We had a battle to fight and a battle to win. I never thought about sending my son to some clinic for psychological counseling or drug rehabilitation. I knew that Jesus and the power of His blood were our only hope. Knowing that God was on our side in this war removed the discouragement and hopelessness.

My husband and I did all that we could do. We loved, prayed, went to court, visited him in the jail, and he still rejected us. He would tell us, "Mom, my homeboys will get me out." He wanted nothing to do with us. I knew he was tripping! I knew this was not my son. Someone else had taken over, his mind was so detached from us; he did not respect us, love us, nor even consider us as his family. He was part of another kingdom, and it was not the kingdom of God.

The courts probated him to a Christian Drug Rehabilitation in another state. He was there a year. Nov. 1999 to Nov. 2000. They worked during the day washing cars and church service during the night. It sort-of rehabilitated him but did not bring total deliverance. He came back home and deliverance came in 2003.

Yet, we continued to pray. His older sisters prayed fervently, his grandmothers prayed diligently, his uncles prayed. Consistent prayer made me courageous, confident, and more assured that God would come through and work things out for good; not just for Kirk Jr. and me, but for all involved.

I began to see things differently. I noticed I wasn't worrying anymore. I started hearing God speak to me more and more. The Holy Spirit started telling me how to pray for him and what to pray. I found words coming out of my mouth during prayer like, "Father show Kirk, Jr. himself?" and "Father, I know there is nothing too hard for you to do." Even in the natural, the condition got worst, but God can comfort like no other. I began looking at Kirk, Jr. like he was a sick patient in the hospital. (He was -- sin sick). I saw him through God's eyes. I was a loving, understanding mom, but I also had to take a step back to let God do the work. My husband and I started praying and fasting more. I believe in blessed oil, and I would pour it on his head when He was sleeping. We showed him God's love and patience. Real, unconditional love is what it takes to forgive and endure with others.

It drew me and my husband closer to each other because we had to teach the other 7 of our children not to be angry with Kirk, Jr. If he stole their car or stole their jewelry to pawn, they needed to forgive. They learned to pray for him and love him. We had to make them see that he needed help and he "knew not what he was doing" because that was not the child I gave birth to, nor the sibling that they loved. There was a stranger living inside of him occupying his body. God did an amazing work. I had to realize that there is nothing to hard for God to do. He is King of Kings and Lord of Lords.

But the grace of God brought us through all the challenges and did a glorious salvation, redemption, and cleansing in Kirk Jr. I am so happy now. I am also proud of him maintaining and fighting the good fight of faith. Kirk, Jr. now works in ministry full-time; preaching and counseling many people. His understanding about the Kingdom of God is outstanding! He is now Pastor, Prophet and Apostle Kirklin Cross, Jr. who is living proof of God's redemptive power working in us, even when we don't think we want it. God can do a work in our children if we submit to Him and let Him do it His way. God did "exceedingly and abundantly above all that we could ask or think." Hallelujah! God is true to his Word! Amen!

"Give your children to God, train them in the ways of God. The word will take root in them and produce a harvest. God is not slack concerning his promises." - 2 Peter 3:19.

Signed,
An Overcomer

I SURVIVED:
Abuse

WHO IS SHE?
And in all honesty, I still don't know.
I started out in humble beginnings growing up in the great state of South Carolina. My biological mother left me to live in Washington, DC after my father was murdered in the neighborhood pool hall over 50 cents from what I was told. My daddy died when I was 4 years old so I only have two vivid memories of him, one being he was the local trash man and I remember seeing him ride down the street on the back of the trash truck and the second time was him lying a casket.

Raised by my maternal grandparents, who took me to church, teaching me about Jesus Christ. I was a member of the Youth usher board, Youth choir, and the Girl Scouts at my childhood church.

I experienced being molested the first time around 9 years old by a female neighbor who was allowed to sleep over at my grandparents' home and the second time I was 10 years old by a deacon who attended my childhood church. Of course I didn't tell because I didn't understand what was going on and the deacon told me not to tell. I left South Carolina at the age of 11 by Greyhound bus alone to live with my mother in Washington, DC and on that Greyhound bus I experienced my third bout of molestation by a stranger still not understanding what was going on.

I finally arrived to the "Chocolate City" and I had never seen so many colored (many colors) people all in one place. I remember my mother taking me to the National Mall where the Monument is located to fly kites and 4th of July festivities. To the Lincoln House to drink Shirley temples and shop on the infamous F street, NW. To this little country girl, being exposed to the big city was exciting. Soon it would be what the enemy thought to be tragic. In August of 1977, my grandfather had a stroke and I went back to SC to see him in the hospital and I remember when he saw me, he smiled, no words. I left the hospital to go to my former elementary school to see my former teachers, I went in to see my music teacher Ms. Baker. We visited briefly, she stepped out of the room for something and I went into her purse and stole a dollar just because. I left the school to go back to my grandparents' home and as soon as I got there, I was told that my grandfather had died. Now in my 12-year-old mind, I thought had I not stolen that dollar from Ms. Baker, he would still be alive. And this caused me to think I was no good to anybody.

From the age of 12 to 15, I was molested by my mother's then boyfriend, which created a spirit of promiscuity. I did not know I was pregnant until I was 8 months taking no vitamins, no checkups, etc. and I gave birth to a HEALTHY baby girl the very next month, I was 15 years old in the 11th grade. I did not know who the father of my child was due to the illicit sexual activity, my mother made me go to court to test the last male I slept with to find out he was not the father of my child. I had to backtrack to find her father. I start doing drugs, smoking cigarettes, drinking alcohol, hanging out in the streets with my so-called friends, having <u>unprotected</u> sex with all types of men. Still having no clue of what's going on, I was determined to finish high school and I did graduate with my high school diploma at the age of 17.

    I was leaving a club I was about seventeen and a stranger offered me a ride home, he raped me, took me home and I still didn't tell. Around the age of 18-19, I started working in a local bar as a waitress where I met a man who was thirteen years older than me and I thought he was my savior. He bought my drugs, we were sleeping in various hotels, having my child with me because I had to be with him. He treated me like a princess until I found out he had another family. I realized I was the young side piece and things quickly turned for the worst. He became abusive mentally and physically. He would embarrass/belittle me by making me sit in his car nude while he was outside of the car drinking with his buddies. He was a raging alcoholic and that's when he would beat me. On one occasion he beat me so that I had two black eyes and he showed me around like a trophy. He forced me to do things to make him feel powerful over me. Threats on the regular. Threats to leave me, threats to cut my face up with a fork saying he would make sure nobody would want me but him. Having complete control over my mind, my body and my spirit! He would lie to me just because he knew I'd believe everything he said. He threatened me not to go to my sister's wedding. He said if I went, he would leave me and of course I didn't go and that still hurts me to this day that I chose him over my sister. The first time I became pregnant by this man I had a miscarriage and I saw my baby (which looked like a glob) outside on the ground the next morning not knowing what happened until I went to the hospital several days later. My mother, at the request of her boyfriend kicked me and my child out in the street. The night she kicked us out we stayed behind the apartment building in the grass. I was up all night scared with a knife in my hand protecting my child. We literally slept in different places for a week until I went to the welfare building in Prince George's County and they put us in a hotel for a short time. I didn't have any money and I didn't know that the hotel was supposed to give us $18 a day for food. The only thing I could give my child was apples because that's all I had and we ate apples for 3 days until I found out about food stipend from the hotel. We were officially homeless! I sought assistance in DC and was placed in temporary shelter. We were in the shelter the first time for about a year and this man got an apartment for us to live in, that didn't last my child and I had to return to the shelter where we resided for another 18 months. During those 18 months I was able to be gainfully employed and able to obtain decent housing for the first time, and of course I allowed him to move in my one bedroom apartment.

The abuse continued and I got pregnant again at the age of 23 years old to be informed that I was carrying twins. I had just started working a housekeeping job and I had to quit because of the pregnancy. He never worked a regular job, always had a hustle. Having to depend on welfare to support myself and soon to be three children. I had a traumatic experience while pregnant with my twins, my middle sister died of the AIDS virus three days before the twins were born. I remember my maternal grandmother came to hospital to see the twins and she stayed until the funeral of my sister and she said to my oldest sister and my mother, there is something special about "Lee Lee", the next time I saw my grandmother she was in a casket. After her death in 1991, I continued to be reckless, having no moral conscience just existing without identity. I remember my mother saying to me, "You ain't no Walker no more." And I'm left thinking well I don't have anybody who wants me.

My oldest sister was the only one in my world that I felt loved me unconditionally and when she was diagnosed with Lou Gehrig's disease, I didn't know what that was, all I knew she was in a wheelchair and she could not walk anymore. She loved my children when I didn't know how to as a young abused single mother. When she died in January 1996, I was devastated beyond comprehension. How can God do this to me? Not her! She was the only one I felt I had love from. I never had anyone to protect me from the world. Every man I slept with I was looking for my father. I didn't understand how I could have been so worthless and unwanted. I would see my mother be abused physically and mentally by my molester and I thought it was acceptable. No one to protect me! My only brother was a good man but he was in and out of the prison system, drug abuser and no one to show him what a man should be and when he died in January 1999 also from the AIDS virus handcuffed to a hospital bed at DC General Hospital, I had no one left.

I had no immediate family, my relationship with my mother was estranged for the lack of a better word and I was still in a mentally abusive relationship with the father of my twins.

I enrolled in the WELFARE TO WORK program under the Barry Administration, where I became gainfully employed with the DC Government for 26 years, now able to provide for my children. LIFE was getting better!

Realizing Jesus was calling me higher and I became an active and faithful member of Anna Johenning Baptist Church where I met my husband of 20 years, Deacon Brian Coley. What's amazing about this marriage, first he was definitely NOT my type and secondly, I wanted to get married because I wanted to have sex and not be in trouble with God! As it progressed through much hardships, ups, downs, to end in divorce after 13 years. I was devastated because here I am again nobody wants me. I remember walking out of the court room going into the bathroom and cried until my face turned red because I simply didn't understand what was WRONG with me? I went on with my life only to see him every week at church. I tried to see someone else which didn't work because, I wasn't the dating type and he wasn't who I saw myself being with for various reasons. Something rekindled after 2 years of being divorced and we remarried in 2009 and we are still together growing in GOD'S grace!

Anna Johenning Baptist Church is now The Temple of Praise Church. During my tenure of 25 years I learned of my calling to minister. I was selected to be ordained as a deaconess in 2009 and in the same year God's grace was extended, I was able to obtained a Masters Degree in Public Administration, Non-profit Management from Southeastern University, Washington, DC. And in 2011, I progressed to a licensed minister under the great tutelage of Bishop Glen A. Staples.

During my tenure with Bishop Staples and The Temple of Praise, I learned different aspects of ministry, which included servant leadership skills, managerial skills, teaching Youth and Young Adult classes, life skills, how to effectively study the Bible using various techniques. My spirit man continued to grow as I learned to study God's Word for myself and with all of this exposure I was fortunate to obtain an Associate's Degree in Biblical Studies, a Bachelor's Degree in Ministry, a Master's Degree in Ministry to finally obtain my Doctorate Degree in Ministry from Andersonville Theological Seminary located in Camilla, Georgia.

Also receiving certificates from University of Phoenix School of Theology. (Refresher courses)

After much prayer and defying the spirit of fear, I believed Jesus when He said to me, Lean not to your own understanding but in all your ways acknowledge Me and I will direct your paths. This has progressed me to where I am currently serving under the great ministry of The Gathering at Forestville {formerly Jabbok Ministries} where Bishop Donald A. Wright introduced and continues to expose me into the higher dimensions of The Spirit. I have never experienced this, here is where the ministry of Marvellousity has come to fruition.

I am purposed for THE GLORY OF GOD and SO ARE YOU! FIND CHRIST, FIND PURPOSE!!!

God has saw fit to allow me to be a part of the GREAT cloud of witnesses ONLY for HIS GLORY and I say to you, that with GOD all things are possible – Luke 1:37

BE ENCOURAGED!!!!!

Signed,
An Overcomer

I SURVIVED:
Addiction

As an Africa American female growing up in Southeast Washington D.C., I was exposed to the horrors of addiction early. There were drug transactions in broad daylight, addict's spewed over fire barrels, drunks stammering down the street, panhandlers on the corner begging for coins to get their next fix, and women scantily dressed looking for their next victim. Empty beer bottles, plastic baggies and drug paraphernalia lined the streets. In the 80's crack cocaine was just beginning to emerge and had become an epidemic. I watched as people I knew and loved fell victim to the debauchery. I would look with distain, glaring in judgment. Puzzled about the fascination; wondering why anyone would smoke crack. I saw firsthand the devastation crack left in its wake. How could such a small piece of white substance, have such a hold on people? It didn't make sense to me. Ignorantly I said to myself; "I could never be like them; I will never smoke that stuff"......not realizing that I would eventually become like those addicts I had seen in the neighborhood. **Mathew 7:1-3** *says, judge not, that you be not judged, for with the judgment you judge, you shall be judged, and with the measure you meet, it shall be measured unto you again.*

I was raised in the church. I got saved and was baptized at a young age. I felt God's nudge early and desired to be used of God. I was filled with the Holy Ghost and sang in the church choir for much of my youth. Reared in a strict and staunchly disciplined household; like most, I had to be in the house before street lights came on. I was forbidden to date and not allowed to talk to boys on the phone. I envied my peers who were dating, partying, drinking and living "the fast life". I was curious, it appealed to me. It seemed fun and appeared glamorous.

I suffered from low self-esteem as a young girl. I did not feel good enough or pretty enough. I was dark-skinned and ruddy with short hair. I was bullied at school and called a black grease monkey (my mother would lick my eyebrows with her spit and grease me down with Vaseline) before I left for school every morning. The blacker the berry the sweeter the juice, my mother would say, as I recalled the taunts of my peers for being so dark-skinned. I developed an inferiority complex; believing other girls, especially the light-skinned girls, were prettier. At least it seemed that way because they got all the attention. I had not learned to love myself. I didn't know I was fearfully and wonderfully made. I didn't feel acknowledged or validated; as a result, I craved attention. I needed to be noticed. I wanted attention; especially from boys. I needed to be affirmed. I looked for tangible love from the opposite sex. Any sign of affection corralled me. I became intoxicated by the cat calls, the whistles and any jester or sign that I was noticed. Despite my Christian upbringing and the strict rules of my mother's house, I was enticed and lured into the world. As a youth, I dressed provocatively to elicit attention and validation. In my defense, I was not mature enough to avoid youthful pleasures, therefore, availed myself to the sinful proclivities.

The absence of a father figure deprived me of a true understanding of how women should be loved and treated. Of course, I was not a woman, just a little girl. Armed with false information and completely unprepared, I became sexually active very early; assuming this was a way to get attention and be loved. Young and naïve, I ignorantly believed that my greatest asset was between my legs. Needless to say, I learned quickly that sex would not guarantee commitment. It would not make him want me or even stay after the dirty deed was done.

Thirsty and desperate to be viewed as desirable and attractive, I entered relationships seeking approval, only to get rejection. After having my first abortion at 14, I met a young man who would eventually become my husband 5 years later.

I had been bitten by the love bug; at least I thought it was love. It was more lust with a twist of strong like. I had taken a ride on the wild side and parked in the alley of disgrace and disrepute. The rules of my momma's house had become too stringent. I thought I was grown, or as my mother would say; "I started smelling myself" Not long after my sophomore year of high school, I left home and moved in with my boyfriend. Armed with a fake ID and a thirst for the fast life, I lived life as an adult; drinking, smoking, partying, going to strip clubs and hanging with people much older than I. By the age of 17, I had a second abortion and was now experimenting with powder cocaine. I told myself it was only social use. It was fun! It was harmless! And, of course; the biggest lie of all; I could stop whenever I wanted to. I minimized my use at first, but, I was addicted. It didn't take long before my tolerance had built and I needed more to get the same effect. Before I knew it, I had graduated to smoking crack cocaine. I thought I was using drugs, but drugs were using me to lie, cheat, and steal. My survival skills weren't as sharp as I thought. I was living hand to mouth. My drug use took precedence over everything. Using drugs had become my everyday life. Nothing else mattered but finding ways and means to get the next fix.

At the age of 19, and six months pregnant with my first child, I was in full active addiction. Unable to **STOP** using, I was **STUCK** using. One night after an all night binge, I returned home and was met by an armed robber who had broken into my apartment. He put a gun to my head and threatened to rape me; (while pregnant). He ransacked my apartment looking for money and drugs. Afraid for my life, I called on the name of Jesus. Surprisingly, the name JESUS alone caused such a reaction in him; literally, his eyes bulged and sweat began to pour down his forehead. He started to rant in a quiet undertone "this is the wrong (superlative) house; "LET ME OUT OF HERE" the gun man headed for the front door, walked out, and I survived. Thank God demons tremble and fear at the name of Jesus.

Needless to say, like the prodigal son, I returned to the church; renewed my commitment to God and begin to seek God for direction and purpose for my life. By the grace and mercy of God, my child was born with no birth defects or signs of drugs in his system. Remorseful and repentant, I unabashedly sought God for a sense of value and worth. God did a quick work. I was ordained evangelist and soon after installed as pastor. I got married and from that union came four beautiful children. Life was good!!! I was focused, determined and on fire for God. I worked in the church and gave myself to ministry. And then the unthinkable happened. I relapsed.

After 10 years clean and as newly installed pastor, I had returned to my vomit (Proverbs 26:11). Initially, I believed it was a faull that I could overcome; until I kept falling. The malady had returned with a vengeance. I tried to stop using but I could not, so I kept using. For a while I minimized the effects this lapse had on my life. After all, I was an adult, able to make my own decisions and I wasn't as bad as others. Needless to say, I was deceived and delusional. I was a mess.

I know what you're thinking; how can you go back after being delivered; where you truly delivered? ***Galatians 5:1, stand fast in the liberty wherewith Christ has made you free and be not entangled again in the yoke of bondage.*** Despite knowing the word of God, I chose to take that first hit. The shear ignorance of me to think I could continue to smoke crack on a daily basis and still preach on Sunday morning. Shamefully, I tried. I tried to hide the contamination of the world. It wasn't long before the wear and tear of addiction was visible. My relapse was evident to the saints. ***Numbers 32:23 says; be sure your sins will find you out.*** Not only did my relapse become public, my life had taken a turn for the worst. I had become prey for the enemy. Sluggish and worn was the outer shell that presented itself at church on a weekly basis. Tired and lifeless was the inner man that was crying out for help. My commitment to God had waned. The spirit had left me; or so I thought. A dark cloud of despair had overshadowed any sense of being. I had surrendered to my disease.

Eventually, I chose crack over Christ. I walked away from the church, from the ministry, and everything I had come to love. The things I didn't walk away from, were taken; namely, my children. Literally, everything I had worked to obtain went up in a puff of smoke (pun intended). I lost my home, resigned a great job and would spend the next year chasing a ghost. It was certainly not the HOLY GHOST. Quite the contrary, I was chasing a ghost that would haunt me. A ghost that would invade my space, hijack my dreams and steal my joy. The ghost of addiction past had come to thwart my future and literally take my life. I was waist deep in the pit of despondency. I was lost and wandering in a wilderness;

backslidden and broken. But the word of God was in me, and the spirit of God gnawed at my flesh to turn. ***Romans 7:23-25 says, but there is something else deep within me, in my lower nature, that is at war with my mind and wins the fight and makes me a slave to the sin that is still within me. In my mind I want to be God's willing servant, but instead I find myself still enslaved to sin.*** I wanted to be free, but I couldn't find the strength to put the crack pipe down. High and literally subconscious most nights, I could still hear **HIS voice saying; shall we continue in sin that grace may abound God forbid. (Romans 6:1).** The Spirit was willing, but the flesh was weak (Mathew 26:41). I knew I needed to do something different lest I die at the hands of this insidious disease.

I attempted to enter treatment; however, while completing the intake exam, I was rushed to the Prince Georges hospital. I had smoked so much crack cocaine, my kidneys were failing. Honestly, I knew something was wrong because my feet were black and there was blood in my urine. I simply couldn't stop using long enough to seek medical attention. I was hospitalized for 7 days, only to call the dealer to the hospital so I could take a hit in the parking garage of the hospital. Once released from the hospital I went back to using. Horror and sorrow filled my life; dejected, isolated, and out of place I lived the "street life" held up in motels, and crack houses, trying to hustle, but getting high on my own supply. Honestly, I was my best customer. I kept giving myself credit. I was taking victims and turning tricks. While in the streets, caught up in the grips and chasing the next high, I was raped. I thought I was street savvy, but the streets had swallowed me up and spit me out like a spoiled piece of meat. I was out of place. I didn't belong. I resisted the constant nudging and the still small voice of God to surrender and return to my first love.

I lost everything, but I knew how to pray! I remembered preaching ***Jeremiah 3:14; Return backsliding children, for I am married to you.***

I knew that although I had left God he had not left me; and even though I was lost, HE knew exactly where I was and HIS mercy would find me there. God had a way of escape for me (I Corinthians 10:13). What most would call an arrest, I called a rescue. God used the Prince Georges County police department as a way of out. I was arrested in a drug raid and was facing 1 year in prison. By the grace and mercy of God, I was given three years' probation and the opportunity to go into treatment. I entered a 28 day facility and then a long-term residential treatment facility, not realizing it was a set up. God would use this relapse and all of its wreckage for my good (Romans 8:28).

Unbeknownst to me, crack addiction and its horrid experiences would be the impetus for a career in addictions counseling. God was rebuilding the ruin; giving me beauty for my ashes. By God's grace, I was introduced to Narcotics Anonymous. I began attending meetings and became acquainted with people who were not using. People whose experience was much like mine. One day at a time, God was renewing my strength. Active in N.A, I began giving back what was so freely given to me; hope and a new way of life. Free from the degradation of addiction, and up from the abyss of the sunken place. I rededicated my life to Christ, joined a local church in the Gaithersburg area and began rebuilding. ***Romans 11:29 says, God's gifts and His calling are irrevocable (NIV).*** It wasn't long before I was speaking at meetings, recovery anniversaries, and other events sharing the message of hope and recovery. Early in recovery, I was hired at Oxford House World Service, which provides sober living for people in recovery. I worked as a residential counselor at Avery House for Women and Children (the very facility I lived in). All of a sudden, just like that, my purpose had been revealed. He had been preparing me to carry out his plan in my life. To give back and work with women who were just like me; lost and addicted. I volunteered at shelters, treatment centers, rehabs, halfway houses, and prisons sharing the message of hope, restoration and recovery.

God used the mess of my life to develop the message of my life. Addiction was simply a backdrop for a message of restoration and recovery. ***"For I will restore you to health and I will heal you of your wounds,' declares the LORD, because they have called you an outcast, saying: "It is Zion; no one cares for her (Jeremiah 30:17).*** God had taken me through a life of addiction and trauma to be a beacon of light and a way out for those who are still lost in the darkness. I survived addiction, today I thrive in recovery. I survived rape, today I thrive in relationship with him. I survived low self-esteem and insecurity; today I live in a secure place with him.

Because of God's mercy and his mighty hand of deliverance, I am not the crack-head I used to be. The old things are passed away and all things are new. Further, I am no longer haunted by the guilt and shame of my past. **Psalms 119:71 says;** It was good that I was afflicted; that I may learn his statues. My past indiscretions and failings were all necessary tools to prepare me for my destiny. Every scar and every wound was a prop in the hands of a master builder. **Psalms 119:67** *says; before I was afflicted I went astray, but now I keep your word.* Living in my purpose, 18 years free from crack cocaine addiction. I stand in that liberty where Christ has made me free. As a pastor, I always felt a call to counseling and was drawn to counseling families and couples. Today, I work with families suffering with substance use disorders as a certified addictions counselor (CAC-1) and Licensed Graduate Professional Counselor (LGPC). What the enemy meant to kill me, God used to make me. Though the road to recovery was rifted with bumps and bruises, I didn't die. I SURVIVED.

I am alive in Christ Jesus; and the life that I now live in the flesh, I live by the faith of the son of God who loved me and gave himself for me. I am grateful to God for his unmerited favor.

Some may be asking, why share my story? Why be so transparent? I share because my story is one of victory. I survived…many have not! Mine is a story of recovery. Unfortunately, some do not recover. I am restored. I lived to tell the story, I am evidence, living proof that you can recover. You can recover all that was lost and/or stolen in the battle with addiction. I share these intimate details to illustrate and illuminate the human side of addiction, of its perfidious hold, and of the liberty and freedom from which I have survived from this horrifying disease.

P.S. If you are dealing with an addiction of any kind be it (drugs, alcohol, sex, pornography, gambling, or food), be encouraged to know that God is a deliverer. It does not matter, what you use, or how much you use. You can be free from bondage and healed from brokenness. There is nothing too hard for God. Call on God. He will help you. He is a present help in trouble. READ: I Corinthians 10:13, Psalms 50:15, James 4:7,

If you need help, **http://drughelpline.org/**, (844) 289-0879

Let us pray!

Father, we ask that you destroy every yoke of bondage and set every captive free. Bring complete and total deliverance from the strong hold of addiction and set at liberty them that are bound, In Jesus Name. Amen.

Signed,
An Overcomer

I SURVIVED:
Depression

I was born in Cheverly, Maryland, and raised in Washington, D.C.. I lived in the inner city where crime, poverty and hopelessness was the norm. My strong mother raised my siblings and I, refusing to succumb to her surroundings and fighting to create a better life for us. She succeeded, but it came with a cost.

I grew up in church. I was saved and baptized at the tender age of nine years old. I did it because I believed it was the right thing to do, and my grandma said so. I served on the Youth Usher Board and sang in the children's choir. I later joined my mother's church. Knowing everything about church that there was to know, I somehow always felt like something was missing. I never felt like I fit or belonged. I fought tirelessly to fit in and to be a part but just couldn't do it.

Aside from fitting in, I was also trying to understand, for many years, why multiple men, who I was supposed to trust, sexually violated me. I also questioned why my "unknown" father wasn't in my life and learned later that it was to protect me. I often asked myself "What's wrong with me?" These events and contemplations pushed me into a dark place that I gradually believed was normal.

After the abuse stopped, I built walls to protect myself. The thought of allowing someone to get too close bothered me. I did not want anyone to know my shame or to see my reality because I defined myself by my abuse and scars. I was damaged goods — violated and unclaimed by the men who were supposed to make me feel safe. My attitude toward relationships with men was poisoned and jaded. I had no real understanding of how to maintain a loving, caring relationship with a man once I didn't and couldn't trust them.

Unhealed, I married in 2005 while seven months pregnant with my son. I walked down the aisle, feeling as big as a house. I was ashamed and embarrassed — a spectacle. With many doubts, I married because I wanted to give my baby what I didn't have — a two-parent family. With all the joy that came from his birth, I still found myself in that very dark place.

It was almost as if a dark cloud hovered over me, and I would cry for hours on end, not wanting to move or get up and care for my baby. I know that sounds like postpartum depression, and it was. Beyond counseling and the support of family, this darkness seemed very familiar to me, like an old lover who knew me and I knew him. I'd go to church, get prayer, fall out, shout, dance and believe that God would take away the bad feelings. I expected them to fall off, so I wouldn't have to deal with them. I was hoping they would magically disappear.

For a while, I was great, feeling happy and free; only to realize, I was still bound. The darkness didn't fall off or disappear! It was waiting for me to put it on like a robe and slippers after every shout, dance and falling out. I didn't want to acknowledge this darkness; I only wanted to believe it didn't exist. Unfortunately, I soon returned to it because it was all I knew.

Fast-forward to 2007 when I experienced a very public church divorce. I felt sad and lonely but still managed to get out of bed for all three church services each Sunday. I was still singing in the choir, serving, and attending church meetings because that's what I was told to do. It helped me function; it kept me busy; but it didn't allow me to address my new reality. I was moving and pushing, but not healing. I avoided dealing with the added tragedy and grief that came with divorce because I had to ignore it. In my mind, confronting it was weak. The potential emotions and tears showed weakness. If I buckled under all of this pressure, then I WAS WEAK.

At this time, my relationship with God was very surface. I knew God's power; I had seen it; but I didn't know it would work for or through me. The way I allowed people to mistreat me was how I defined God's feelings toward me. I questioned, "Why would His power work for me or through me? I wasn't worthy." I relied heavily on those around me to tell me what to do. They were the voice of God in my life, not God himself. When they said to gird myself up and stop crying over the mess I made, or to get myself together because I only wanted attention, or that I was being overly dramatic, I suppressed my gloom and dread, pretending they were nonexistent. When they told me to "pull on the power in me," I wondered, "What power?" I was certain that God would never speak to me because I wasn't important enough, I came from the wrong part of town and I had done the unthinkable. Please don't assume that my advisors were bad people because they're not; they were simply giving me what they knew to be sound wisdom.

By August 2013, I was experiencing a part of life that I had only heard about beforehand: they called it "rock bottom." I lost loved ones, my marriage, my own home and my lucrative job. I was employed for less than what I was accustomed to and could not keep a roof over our heads. Transition after transition, I had never experienced this kind of pain or sadness, and it all happened at once without any breaks. This rock bottom was like a new, fresh hell.

For many years, I hid behind serving in and/or leading several ministries in my local church; but after each service, meeting or church event, I would go home alone and fight unexplainable sadness, insecurity, self-doubt, self-hatred, frustration and anger. I repeatedly questioned whether I would ever be good enough, pretty enough and strong enough, and whether I could ever live up to their expectations.

Would I ever become what I've seen or will I always continue to be good enough to serve and not be minimized by those I serve? Their treatment convinced me that I would never be good enough to accomplish the things that I knew God had called me to and had for me. I eventually realized that I wasn't just emotional; I was depressed, church going, shouting, speaking in tongues, anointed, called, chosen AND DEPRESSED!! SICK WITH DEPRESSION! Depressed, the thoughts of my future gave me anxiety. What future? I thought many times, THIS IS IT! The kind of depression that made me wonder "why am I still here?" "Why stay here?" "Why would God want me?" I was broken! Wearing the "mask", quoting the church clichés but I was dying inside. DYING!

I would go home and cry for hours and even contemplated suicide, even made a few attempts because I felt like no one, including God loved me or really understood what I was experiencing. I felt ashamed to go to anyone because here I am a leader in church but can't control my emotions. I was told that I needed to navigate my emotions, you know get them in check, nothing I was dealing with was that bad, I was unstable and my double mindedness would affect people. I lived a life of fear, torment and panic.

I learned to live with it and hide it to avoid feeling judged, minimized and embarrassed. I learned to be someone else. I developed the ability to show people who I wanted them to see which ultimately resulted in me having NO idea of who I was. I had become a deceiver; solely to hide how broken I was. I developed the inability to show emotions unless I was angry. I was hard, resentful, unforgiving, doubtful, coarse, unapproachable, untrusting and callus. I no longer trusted the soul of anyone and everyone had a motive. Especially men. Some of them I indulged because they were great at numbing me. I questioned everything and would always lean to the negative FIRST. I was pessimistic, envious and jealous of people. Jealous of their freedom because I desired to be free, but I was STUCK!!!

I was ashamed of who I was privately but proud publically. I hated myself! I hated life! I hated the "church" because no one saw how broken I was or they just didn't care. To them I was a commodity of servanthood and I needed to get myself together. I got tired of hearing how anointed I was and how God had a plan for my life. It sickened me! I could care less about how anointed I was and how He'd use me, I was trying to make it to the next minute without having a breakdown. I didn't care about the anointing, I wanted to know how the hell do I navigate through life! I wanted to know how to get FREE!

My defining moment was in 2013 when I obeyed the voice of God and transitioned to another ministry. Not because my previous church was bad but because it was time to heal, to grow, to meet myself and that's exactly what happened. The process began in August 2013 when I lost my home and was evicted. I stood in the middle of the courtyard looking at all of the things I had worked so hard for laying in the grass. It broke me, but I made myself pull it together. I slept on my best friend's couch with my child for 5 months. During that time, I lost a dear friend and relative, partially because of the same stress and lie I'd been living.

The lie of everything being ok and I really am happy. I was working 12-15 hour days just to avoid dealing with all of what I was feeling and the stress behind it. I was not sleeping; I was not eating. I was just running on programming. I continued this pattern until October of 2013. I was walking down the hallway with my brother and they told me I was talking randomly, nothing I said was making any sense. They took my son into the house and my brother looked at me and said let it fall apart.

Break! I was told I said "I'm fine" and that I had to get in the house to take care of my child. I eventually collapsed and started screaming and crying. I heard my brother in my ear telling me to cry and "let it all out!" and he held me up and let me cry in his arms. I was tired, I was weak, I was exhausted, I WAS SICK! I learned how to live with it. It was my normal but I believe God allowed this moment to move me into my freedom.

Sick of keeping up appearances, sick of pretending to be ok, sick of lying, sick of hurting, sick of hiding, I was sick! I realized I had no thoughts of the future because I had no idea who I was. I had no idea I, Ikisha, had a future that God Himself created for me, not the me that everyone wanted me to be, but the me He designed! A free me! Healed me!! A delivered me!! I was sick and the sickness of depression and loss of self-identity caused me to adopt practices that were contrary to who God said I was!

I was lying because I was SICK, I was promiscuous because I was SICK, I was over-eating because I was SICK, I overworked because I was SICK. I did everything I could think of to not have to deal with that deep darkness that was inside of me. Anything to numb it, anything that would make it go away even for a little while. I medicated myself not with drugs but with men, with church, and my career. I just wanted it to stop. I wanted clarity of thought, I wanted peace of mind, I wanted to SLEEP!

Yes, I knew God called me but I didn't care, because at that time the "call" wasn't keeping me. I needed the thing that keeps you. I had come into a place of desiring freedom more than desiring status. I wanted to be free from opinions and thoughts of doom from feeling like I had no future.

My then Pastor saw that. He saw the mask and he allowed me to come to church, sit, and hear God's Word and I began my journey of freedom. I had become a slave to unforgiveness, bitterness, anger, fear, anxiety, and pride. I had learned to live with this stuff that kept me bound and unable to move in the purpose of God. I was chained to these emotions and thoughts.

I FINALLY surrendered one night at home. I was tired, and worn out. I knew suicide was not an option and I just wanted to be free, so I began to worship Him, I began to tell Him how much I loved him and how I needed him, I told Him how tired I was and how I just wanted to be free. I began to release to God and I heard these words, "I have always wanted you, I have always loved you." Imagine lying in bed wanting to be held and made to feel safe and the Lord comes to where you are and holds you. That was the first time I felt safe. I rejected a serious relationship with God because of fear, because again I had been mishandled by men that I was supposed to be able to trust. So trusting God was no exception. In my mind, He was a man but that night was a defining moment. Just me and God. As I grew in grace, He taught me through prayer and study how to face those demons that had tormented me for years; He made me acknowledge and held my hand through it. He gave me space to talk about how badly it hurt me. I would go to the Father and cry, sometimes screaming only having the words "it hurts", "they hurt me", "where were You" not knowing that those cries and screams were healing me. The Lord taught me that tears are not a sign of weakness, but a sign of strength.

He was healing me because I acknowledged that the pain was there. I learned that although He knew anyway, He wanted me to trust Him enough to bring it to Him, to give Him the pain and shame I had held on to for so many years. He wanted it. He wanted it all. So I gave it to Him, sometimes being hesitant because I was afraid He would throw me away because I was so damaged.

When I realized He loved me and would never throw me away; I found myself giving Him everything. Things I had suppressed so deep inside of me, I forgot they were there but they were the reason, the reason I was SICK! This birthed the intercessor. After a year, my Pastor felt the release from God and loosed me to pray and intercede. In 2015, I was licensed to preach the gospel and affirmed as a prophet in the Lord's church; ONLY after I sat and allowed God to heal me. My Pastor allowed me to SIT! Not lead, not serve, he let me heal. I will forever be grateful to him for that.

In February 2016, after ending an unhealthy relationship, I met someone who would change my life. He was interested in learning who I was and not who I once pretended to be. I was able to share my faults and what was at one time my shame and he showed God's heart for me. He loves me, encourages me, protects me, and he vowed to do this for the rest of our lives.

I am now married, with four beautiful children and I stand alongside my husband as the Senior Leader of the Emmanuel Kingdom Fellowship Church in Cleburne, TX.

Today I am Free! I am walking in freedom! I live in freedom! I am walking out my healing. I live in my healing. I breathe in my healing. I am healed in my mind. I am healed in my soul. I am healed in my spirit. I am healed in my emotions. God has healed me. God is healing me. I have no fear of the future because my future is in God's hands and because I know Him. He loves me and His promises are over my life. So I can walk into the future with NO FEAR! I now understand and know that I am loved, I am worthy, and I am important to God and SO ARE YOU!

Signed,
An Overcomer

www.ingramcontent.com/pod-product-compliance
Lightning Source LLC
Chambersburg PA
CBHW070051120526
44589CB00034B/1973